D1288599

WOOD INLAY

WOOD INLAY
Art and Craft

Joseph Forgione/Sterling McIlhany

Demonstration Photographs by Alfred Russo

An Art Horizons Book

Van Nostrand Reinhold Company
New York Cincinnati London Toronto Melbourne

A*

Library of Congress Catalog Card No. 72-9723
ISBN 0-442-22423-0

Printed by Jolly & Barber Ltd, Rugby.

Design Consultant: Milton Glaser

Published in 1973 by Van Nostrand Reinhold Company
A Division of Litton Educational Publishing, Inc.
450 West 33rd Street, New York, N.Y. 10001

16   15   14   13   12   11   10   9   8   7   6   5   4   3   2   1

Also by the authors:
Art as Design: Design as Art by Sterling McIlhany (1970)
Banners and Hangings by Norman Laliberté and
Sterling McIlhany (1966)

Frontispiece:
Chess board, 30 x 30
inches, by Joseph
Forgione. Six varieties
of wood block and,
mostly, veneers were used
to create an impressive
game board. Each square
of the checkered surface
is composed of four
triangular pieces, which
produces an optical
illusion of depth in
space. The heraldic
shields that frame the
board were inspired by
historic and contem-
porary institutions and
individuals. Each emblem
is repeated in reverse
value.

Contents

1.
Wood Inlay in Time and Art

Along with stone, wood is the oldest solid medium employed by man for functional and aesthetic forms. By 30,000 B.C. progressive workers had created stone utensils with which they could shape and carve pieces of wood for a variety of uses—from decorative headgear for magical rites and dances to clubs and arrow staffs for war and hunting .

So wood is a basic material, one familiar to the barbaric caveman and used often by the modern craftsman. It is the closest contact we have with the natural world, for like people, trees are related, living forms of seemingly infinite variety.

With the advent of civilization in ancient Mesopotamia and Egypt, wood became a major medium for expression in the arts and crafts. Museum showcases throughout the West contain boxes, religious ornaments and figures, and furniture inserts of inlaid wood patterns. In the earliest examples, especially miniature figures and boxes, cut and inlaid wood pieces are usually set with gemstones and precious metals.

However used, wood inlay evolved as a fine-art form that was employed throughout Classic and Medieval times and reached a stunning climax in the Italian Renaissance. By the 15th century, wood-inlay patterns ranged all the way from family heraldic designs and the geometric chessboard, with its juxtaposed equal squares, to massive palace doors that supported naturalistic mythological figures of woods with many hues, values, and grains. Probably the most famous wood-inlaid doors are those (one reproduced here) within the Ducal Palace at Urbino, Italy, whose life-size allegorical figures were designed by the Florentine genius, Botticelli. The doors are of unique value to today's craftsman because they are a dramatic introduction to the large scale and compelling figurative design that can be achieved with skillful experience and free imagination. As outlined simply in the demonstration series, the basic approach was to begin with a preliminary drawing (called "cartoon"), then to select a number of wood veneers of different shades and decorative grains. The probable traditional technique was to cut the contrasting veneers into separate pieces that matched, in size and shape, the parts of the preliminary cartoon drawing they were to recreate. After all pieces for a single panel were cut to size, they were glued edge-to-edge (like joining fragments of a jigsaw puzzle) onto a heavy wood panel. After all pieces were matched perfectly as a finished climax to the original drawing, the newly inlaid panel was rubbed to a smooth surface and lacquered.

Wood inlay achieved a new character in the 17th and 18th centuries in the hands of skilled furniture designers in France. From their creative genius comes marquetry, or the elegant wood-inlaid furniture that was commissioned by noble families, including the Bourbon kings, for their town palaces and country castles. Desks, cabinets, tables, chairs —occasionally even fine floors—were decorated with abstract and figurative designs. Characteristic of this lavish period, wood inlay was often enhanced by the addition of gold, shells, and ivory.

Another wood-inlay technique still of concern to the contemporary craftsman is the geometric wooden floor. Known in France as parquet, inlaid floors were utilitarian large-scale productions built as functional room decor firm enough to be walked upon by thousands of people: family members, staff, and visitors. As in other inlay projects,   7 today's parquet floors are most often manufactured in modular blocks—and often of synthetic, imitative media. In spite of the availability and ease of application of mass-produced blocks, it is still reasonable and simple to design and construct one's own inlaid floors of independently selected woods and original designs. For example, it is both practical and visually rewarding to create a wood-inlay floor surface for a small room such as an entrance hallway or the area around the hearth of a fireplace or before a window. Such small wooden floor spaces placed over another floor surface can be safely blended into it with quarter-round molding strips.

Resting securely on the earlier developments in Italy and France, the 19th century became largely a period of revival of wood inlay, in both design and technique. As the final reproductions indicate, 20th-century wood inlay embodies the functions and creative approaches peculiar to our time of the abstract in all arts and crafts. From miniature pendants to tables and screens, contemporary designs reflect the modern craftsman's devotion to basic shape and overall pattern. A perfect example is the checkered design. Originally conceived as a portable gameboard, it has become a central theme for wood-inlay art, re-

gardless of its use or size. The checker-top table can be a playing surface if so desired, but it exists primarily as a functional coffee table for decor and drinks or a small dining-room table for regular meals. An inlaid elevator door symbolizes the modern machine age with its constant need to transport people—either horizontally or vertically.

Wood inlay, from its beginnings to today, has served the craftsman as a means for expressing the needs and desires of his time. Whether used in a Renaissance door panel or a contemporary coaster, inlaid wood can be as flexible and expressive a medium as painting and often as durable as stone.

Inlaid Renaissance choir seats by Marti and Pucci, Lucca, Italy. (Photograph courtesy Alinari.)

Detail of palace room with illusionistic wall design of walnut, oak, beech, rosewood, and fruitwoods. Originally from Gubbio, Italy. 15th century. Through the use of perspective, realistic forms, and surface variety, the artist-craftsman achieved the essence of space and a great number of objects on flat, inlaid walls. (The Metropolitan Museum of Art. Rogers Fund, 1939.)

Allegorical figure on a door panel in the studio of Duke Federigo, Urbino, Italy. 15th century. Original design for the door was probably created by Botticelli. The monumental figure with its illusion of three dimensions is typical of the master's work. (Photograph courtesy Alinari.)

Inlaid wood panel from wainscoting of Château de la Bastie d'Urfé, St. Etienne, France. 16th century. A variety of wood grains was used to create the instrument and its surrounding related objects. (The Metropolitan Museum of Art. Gift of the children of Mrs. Harry Payne Whitney in accordance with the wishes of their mother, 1942.)

Above. Detail of wall panels from Flims, Switzerland, composed of walnut, maple, sycamore, and other native woods. 17th century. (The Metropolitan Museum of Art. Rogers Fund, 1906.)

Below. Parquet or wood-inlaid floor in the Hall of Mirrors, Palace of Versailles, France. 1678. (The Bettman Archive.)

Above. English commode in the Adams style inlaid with East Indian satinwood, harewood, pheasant-wood, boxwood, sycamore, mahogany, holly, and thuja. 18th century. (The Metropolitan Museum of Art. Fletcher Fund, 1929.)

Below. French commode of various woods, style of Louis XVI. 18th century. (The Metropolitan Museum of Art. Bequest of Collis P. Huntington, 1926.)

Above, left. Small French storage table of various woods, also brass and bronze. 18th century. (The Metropolitan Museum of Art. Bequest of Catherine D. Wentworth, 1948.)

Above, right. Modern wood inlay with metal stripping, on elevator door in the Chrysler Building, New York. 1920s. (Photograph by Fortune Monte.)

Modern commercial inlaid table top, 36 x 36
inches, in checker pattern. 1970s (Courtesy
Door Store, New York City.)

Tools. *Top:* razor saw. *Left to right:* veneer saw, glue, block plane, home-made knife, long-handle knife, veneer tape, roller, protractor. *Bottom:* ruler for cutting straight lines.

2.
Tools, Woods, and Beginning Project

The project described and illustrated in this chapter is an introduction to basic tools and techniques. The aim is to show that with little or no previous experience you can create a simple, well-designed wood inlay. In order to develop feeling for wood block and, most importantly, veneers, nothing too difficult should be attempted at the start. Therefore, the first project is to cover a small block with veneer. This is an opening step that paves the way for a growing mastery of other, more complex projects.

Tools

1. Knife. Select a wood-carving knife whose handle has the right length and thickness for your grip. Its blade should be a steel one that tapers to a fine point. For easier cutting, the blade should be sharpened by honing it on both sides.
2. Oil stone for sharpening knife. There are many good stones available. Among the best is the India combination stone. The knife should be sharpened

often by placing a few drops of machine oil on the stone and honing the blade back and forth on both sides. Care should be taken to hold the knife almost flat on the stone, always sharpening on both sides to produce a finely-tapered point. The oil stone should be cleaned after each session.
3. Twelve-inch steel rule for cutting straight lines.
4. Cutting board of soft plywood, such as fir or white pine. (Hard plywood would break the point of a knife when it cut through the work and onto the cutting board.)
5. Tapes. Veneer tapes for holding work-in-progress together and masking tape.
6. Contact and rubber cements.
7. Machine oil for sharpening.
Also, for advanced use:
8. Power jig saw.
9. Veneer press for holding glued pieces under pressure.

Woods

In addition to the wood blocks and plywood pieces that are used as bases for inlay, the veneers available are varied and many. The color veneer circle on page 19 indicates by reproduction the many veneers from which one can select when creating a design, be it a simple block or a many-faceted pattern (like the circle itself). Each veneer is different. There is a tremendous range in hues, grains, and values. All can act as reference for future selection in projects and independent works.

Project
Veneer on a Block (pages 21-23)
The first step in this beginning project is to select and cut the pieces of wood to be used. After a 1-inch-thick pine block is cut to a square, 4 x 4 inches, two squares of plain mahogany veneer are cut to 4½ x 4½ inches, and four pieces to 4½ x 1¼ inches.

Next, brush one side of the block and

one side of a 4½ x 4½-inch piece of veneer with fast-setting contact cement. After 30 minutes, the pieces should be ready for gluing together. Place veneer square, with glued side up, on flat work area, and press glued side of block over it, leaving approximately ¼-inch of veneer showing on all sides. A block of this size should adhere evenly and

without difficulty.

Trim off the excess veneer. The ideal tool for this step is a veneer saw, which can be bought at any store that sells veneers. But a good knife, like that illustrated, is an excellent beginning tool. At the start, try not to be impatient: cut slowly, not pressing too heavily with the knife. Cutting with the grain is done

easily all the way from one end of the veneer to the other. However, an important rule to remember: when cutting across the grain with a knife, start at the ends and cut toward the center. After this preliminary trimming is done, repeat the same procedure of gluing and trimming on the other side of the block.

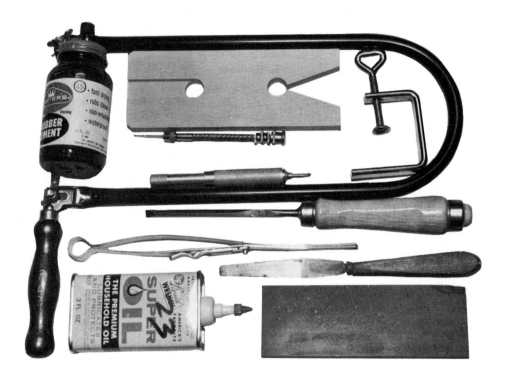

Tools. *Top:* fretsaw. *Within fretsaw:* rubber cement, jig for fretsawing, veneer drill, glue injector, clamp. *Bottom:* chisel, veneer tweezer, palatte knife, oil for sharpening tools, sharpening stone.

Veneers. This circular inlay illustrates the remarkable variety of veneers available to the craftsman. The range of warm and cool colors, light and dark values, and wood grains can be variously combined to create a limitless number of visual effects.

18

19

Power jigsaw. Handle on lower right corner is for hand use – instead of power use. Behind saw is rack with different-size blades.

Below. Home-made veneer press used with slow setting glues and, most often, for flattening buckled veneers. When used for the latter, veneers are moistened with sponge, put between the two pieces of ¾-inch plywood, and clamped by use of bolts and thumbscrews.

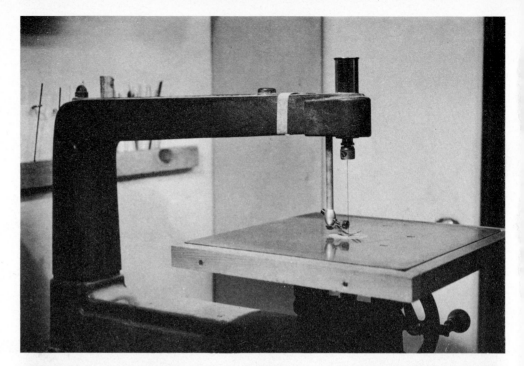

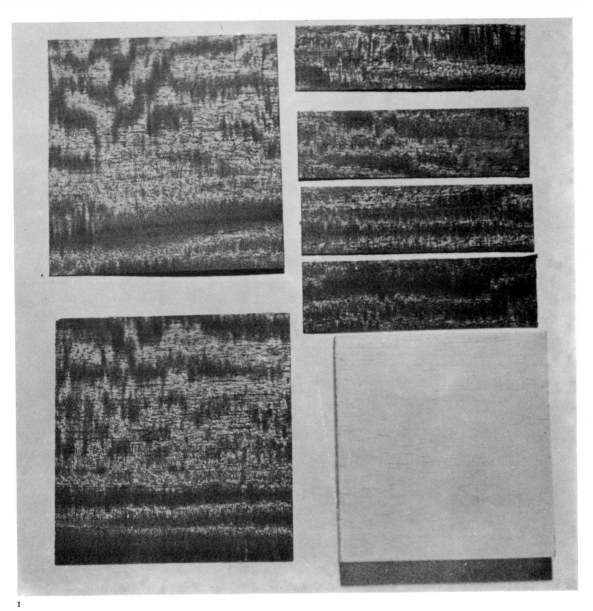

1. Pine block and six strips of mahogany veneer for covering its top, bottom, and sides.

2

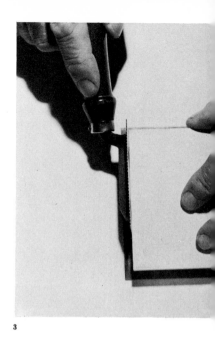

3

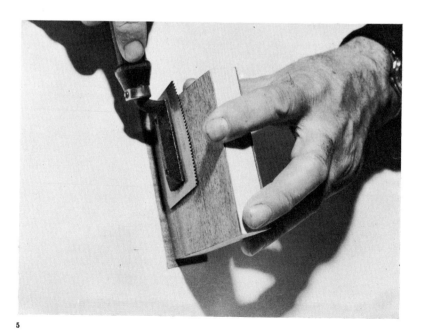

5

6

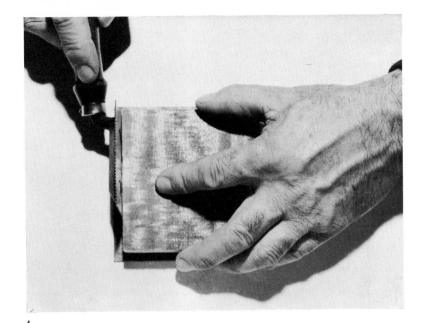

4

2. Block being glued to veneer square.

3. Trimming off excess edges of veneer.

4. Trimming excess edges of veneer glued to other side of block.

5. Trimming veneer strips glued to sides of block with veneer cutter.

6. Finished pine block covered with mahogany veneer.

Geometric square, 8 x 8 inches, by Joseph
Forgione. A richly grained wood texture
framed by bands of light veneer creates a
block of equal value as support for another
object or a small wall hanging.

3.
Panel Design

Panels created by wood-inlay techniques serve several functions. As relatively small forms, like those illustrated here, they can act as trays or supports for vases and other decorative pieces. They can also be hung on a wall or placed on a flat surface to be regarded as individual works of art.

Of special interest to craftsmen and amateurs who gain great pleasure from creating or embellishing useful objects in their own environment are panel sections that act as decorative additions to furniture. Panels can be designed as table tops or chair backs to be added to furniture already at hand or to simple pieces made at home or purchased at a store that sells unpainted and unstained pieces, such as chests and tables, chairs and functional cube boxes, that would be ideal for various-size panel additions.

The most dramatic of all inlay panels are large-scale geometric designs that can be constructed just as the smaller examples, using wood veneer cut with knife and straight edge and mounted on flat plywood panels. Large panels with complex or simple, bold designs can be mounted on doors, made into hinged room-divider screens, or simply placed against a section of the wall to add an elegant, hand-crafted quality to a room.

Rectangular tray, 11½ x 16 inches, by Joseph Forgione. A diagonal, geometric design of high value-contrast veneers. A design so bold and symmetrical could be recreated at large scale for a table top or even a dynamic wall panel.

Table-top, 36-inch diameter, by Louis David. A subtle combination of geometric and free-form shapes produces a flowing pattern which is in accord with the basic, circular shape of the table. (Reproduced courtesy *Craft Horizons*.)

Four eight-sided coasters using a variety of designs, by Joseph Forgione. Two (upper right and lower left) are bold geometric designs similar to the design in the project. The other two use geometric shapes set in irregular patterns.

4.
Advanced Project

Coaster Project

Materials and Procedure

Two pieces of veneer of contrasting colors and values and one piece of ¼-inch plywood are required. Draw the design indicated as accurately as possible— with a 4-inch diameter, and transfer the design onto the plywood cutting. A piece of carbon paper can help.

The grain of the veneer *makes* the design. Running with the grain, cut a few pieces, ½ inch in width, out of each of the contrasting veneers.

Place a strip with one straight edge along *A-E*. A small piece of tape may be used to hold it in place. Using the straight edge ruler, cut from *A* to *1*. These lines may be extended to insure the accurate placing of the metal ruler. Be careful and make light cuts to avoid splitting. Next cut is from *1* to center. This completes the first piece. If the design is symmetrical and the cutting of the first piece accurate, all the parts of the star could be cut by using the first

piece as a template. But perfection is so difficult that it is better to fit one piece at a time.

Next, place a contrasting strip along side of the first piece, which should be secured in place with masking tape, and now make a cut from *A* to *8*, then from *8* to the center. Tape these two pieces together with a very small piece of tape, which should never extend beyond the edges.

The next piece should be placed with edge running along line *B-F*. Slip the side that covers number *1* under the first piece that was cut. The first piece acts as a cutting line from *1* to center. Next, cut from *1* to *B*. Having succeeded in making the first three pieces, the rest of the cutting for the star is carried out in the same manner. You may continue clockwise or counterclockwise as you wish.

Fitting in the Angle Pieces (A-B-1)

Cut strips of veneer about 1½ inches wide. Place one strip running with the

grain along line *A-B*. If you like, these pieces could be of a third veneer, different from the two used for the star. This piece should run under the star. Using the sides of the star, cut from *1* to *A* and from *1* to *B*; this piece should fit snugly. Next, cut from *A* to *B*. Angles *B-2-C*, *C-3-D*, etc., are all cut in the same manner.

Just in case the knife does not run perfectly straight, and this happens once in a while to even the best, one way to straighten is to place a block plane upside down into a vice. Blade must be very sharp, very little cutting edge showing. Before trying on any piece of your work, first test a piece of scrap veneer.

Another method is to glue a piece of fine sandpaper onto a piece of straight board, preferably a piece of plywood about 6 x 6 inches. For best results, glue with contact cement. Follow procedure for all gluing as explained in the veneering of a 4-inch block on page 18.

Cutting of Coaster, Completed Gluing
Brush contact cement on one side of star; other side should be taped to hold pieces together. This took place automatically in the cutting procedure. The star should be pressed onto plywood making sure that it is perfectly bonded. Tap with a hammer, using a block of wood if necessary.

Next, cut pieces of plywood using a *zona saw.* Make sure that the cuts are square. This finished, veneer the bottom of the coaster. Follow same procedure as veneering of 4-inch block; trim excess veneer using knife or *veneer saw.* Now, veneer all the eight edges. Remember to brush on glue evenly and to wait until glue is ready. Follow instructions of manufacturer.

Finishing
Sand with very fine sandpaper. A very good sanding block can be made by wrapping the sandpaper around a block of either cork or styrofoam (polystyrene). When smooth, wipe clean with soft cloth.

Varnish is a very good finish for coasters. Two or three coats should be given with sanding between each coat. After the last coat, it may be polished by using a mixture of one part linseed oil and one part turpentine. Wet the sandpaper with the solution and rub the design with even strokes. Again, wipe clean with a soft cloth.

Many other finishes can be made. A number of books can be referred to on this subject, which can be obtained from establishments that sell veneers.

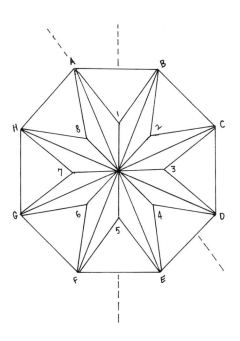

1. Drawing of coaster star design with 4-inch diameter, to be transferred to piece of plywood. Dotted lines ensure a more accurate placing of ruler for straight cuts.

2. Design of star and veneers selected for star coaster. This project is to be done with the use of knife and metal-edge ruler.

3. A block plane can be used to straighten out a poor cut. The blade of the plane should be razor sharp. The amount of the blade projecting over the flat part of the plane should be adjusted for the finest cut possible.

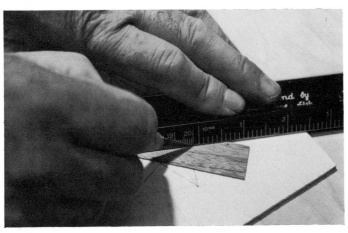

4. First cut. A strip is placed along line *A—E*. Cut from *A* to *1*, then from *1* to the center.

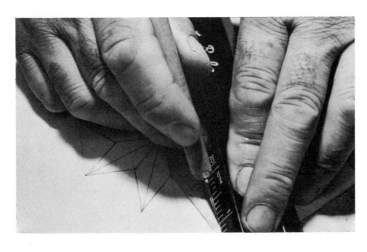

5. Second cut. On this contrasting veneer strip, placed alongside the first piece, cut from *A* to *8* and from *8* to the center.

33

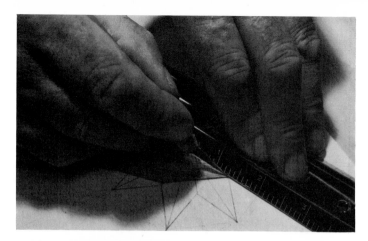

6. Third cut. Another contrasting veneer strip is placed with edge running along line *B—F*. Cut from *1* to center, then from *1* to *B*.

7. Cutting between star points. Care is taken to face the grains in proper directions to achieve contrast among the parts of the star.

8. The previous cut, a large triangle, is placed between points. Star is held together by pieces of veneer tape.

9. All triangles are cut out and put in place. Coaster is taped together and ready for gluing to plywood block.

10. A razor saw is used to shape the outside edges of the star.

11. Contact glue is applied to the backside of the coaster.

12. Finished star coaster. Veneer design is glued onto plywood, which is trimmed to its 8-sided shape.

Opposite Page

Four coasters of geometric design, by Joseph Forgione, made with veneers of different values and grains.

1. Use the veneer drill to make a starting
hole in order to cut the circle in two pieces
of plywood, one on top of the other.

5.
Introducing the Fretsaw
and Power Saw

As the fretsaw might be new and unfamiliar to most people, it is advisable to learn how to use it on a series of ¼-inch or ½-inch thick pieces of plywood. Secure two same-size pieces of plywood. Join them by driving four very fine nails, one on each corner. Onto the plywood surface, pencil a circle for the start. Using a veneer drill or a very fine brad, make a hole within the design and insert the fretsaw blade from the top. The teeth of the saw should point down. The blade is secured into the frame, making sure that there is a certain amount of tension on the blade. The work is done on a fretsaw table which is clamped or secured onto a work table with C-clamps.

The idea of this project is practice in holding the saw perpendicular to the work. Do not use too fine a blade in the beginning; use a 1/0 or 2/0 blade. When the cutting is finished, the cut-out circles from the two pieces of plywood should be interchangeable. If they are not, be very patient and keep trying with other scraps of plywood until the right results are obtained. Remember that the aim is to be able to hold the saw perpendicular to the work. After this is achieved, try the same project again, this time concentrating on always holding the saw in one position, moving the work towards the blade. Use very light strokes, concentrate on keeping the hand very relaxed. As soon as you feel that you can control the saw, proceed with other blades, which come as fine as 8/0. Do a lot of practicing with only two contrasting types of squares. Practice making silhouettes until the saw moves with ease.

After the above is accomplished, you should proceed to some of the kits that are available at veneer stores. This is a very good introduction to the techniques of the inlay picture. The use of different veneers makes the picture. Some stores carry over a hundred different kinds of veneers, which come from practically every part of the world. Just as the artist uses colors for creating a picture, the wood-inlay craftsman uses veneers.

As you work with a fretsaw, you might develop independent ways to work with it. As an example: I hooked up a jig under the table to hold the saw perpendicular to the table. It rides on a shaft and makes it possible to move the saw with just two fingers, thereby leaving the right hand very relaxed. This method also holds the blade steady in one direction. Of course the left hand moves the work.

A favorite is the power jigsaw. I do not use it as a power saw. Rather, I connect a handle on the pulley—which is controlled by the use of the right hand—instead of a motor. This technique makes possible very delicate strokes when working on exceptionally small details, and it also makes possible the use of finer blades, which would break if a motor were attached.

The power saw will handle 3/0 blades, even with the use of the motor. But by using the motor it sometimes becomes difficult to make sharp turns. For this reason I prefer working the saw by hand. (It is also very easy to tilt the saw table at about a 10-degree angle for better fits). When the table is tilted, however, one must be careful to move the work continuously from the start of the cut, making sure that the high part of the bevel is on top. (If the saw should break, you might discontinue the current approach to the work and change its direction, for the fit will be a poor one.)

Some of the kits from England give excellent instructions for cutting—especially with a knife—and for going from step to step in the whole veneer procedure. Their veneers are much thinner than the American, so knife cutting is very possible and quick, especially with the softer veneers. But when cutting the harder veneers such as rosewood, teak, or ebony, the saw is preferable. With some American veneers knife cutting is difficult, therefore slow.

The teeth of a power saw face you and the work is pushed away from you. Therefore, you cut counterclockwise around the piece that is to be inserted into its background.

4. Finished project: *Right:* two pieces of plywood used in fretsaw practice. Square on bottom has pattern of circle marked on it. *Left:* the two squares with cut-out circles interchanged to produce a bold wood inlay.

3. Using fretsaw to cut circle. The saw remains in steady position while the work is gently pushed toward the saw. Right hand moves the saw gently up and down. There should be no forcing, for it results in blade breakage and poor cutting.

Opposite Page

2. Inserting a fretsaw blade into the hole. It is then fastened to a fretsaw and cutting of circle is started. Notice home-made jig for fretsawing. The channel is made to allow the fretsaw to cut perpendicular to the work.

1. Stack of veneers with a pattern on top arranged for multiple cutting. Different kinds of contrasting veneers are used. The cutting procedure is the same as that for cutting the circle. As the parts are cut, they should be placed in a tray for final assembling. The contrasting assembly of veneer pieces should be done as the individual desires.

2. Multi-layer cutting with the power saw. The left hand moves the taped stack, with the design on top, toward the blade.

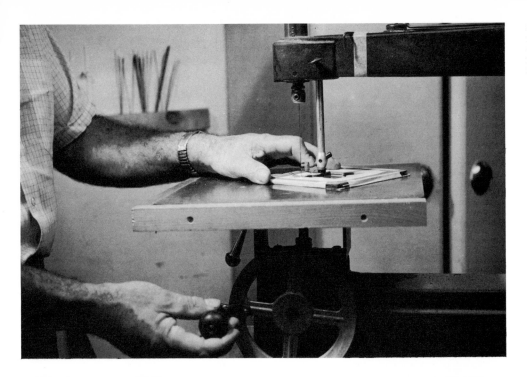

3. Using the power saw in multiple or sandwiched cutting. Notice how the power saw can be an excellent hand tool. The handle placed on the pulley makes fine cutting much easier to control.

4. Assembling cut parts.

5. Cut parts taped together and ready for gluing on reverse side.

6. Reverse side on which glue is applied.

6.
Picture Panels

For many centuries wood inlay artists and their patrons have been fascinated by the creation of illusionistic wooden panels. Palace doors, the backs of choir stalls, even whole walls have been inlaid with intricate scenes of nature and cities, details of room interiors, and towering mythological figures. Less grandiose but of equal skill and beauty are small picture panels that, like paintings, are designed in scale and subject to be hung on a wall as a serious work of art. Like paintings of any media, picture panels can depict any subject or scene desired. Scenes from nature have a special appeal because wood itself is a creation of nature. The wood surfaces of different grain, pattern, and depth of light and shade recall personal encounters with nature in the open air.

Working on a Project of Your Own

When working on a personal project, the knowledge gained from others is always of the greatest importance. Without others we probably would not be working at anything at all. But whatever idea comes to your mind for a project, work at it, work on it; it is yours.

Whatever you undertake, do not make the frequent mistake of being too impatient to finish. Always work slowly, cheerfully, and give yourself a chance. If things seem to go wrong, stop and relax; do something else for a while. Your basic interest in the work will take you back to it with refreshed ideas and skill.

Whether you work from a photograph, a well-known painting, or your own sketch, you must remember that a good inlay is put together just as a good jigsaw puzzle. The pieces are cut the same way but, of course, not intended to fulfil the same function. The aim is not to make a puzzle but to put together different pieces of veneers to create an attractive composition from elements of nature's woods, which you will enjoy looking at and be proud to share with others.

After your preliminary drawing or sketch is ready, you must trace the main outlines in jigsaw fashion. Once that is done, determine the colors by studying the different veneers you have on hand and those that are otherwise available. Unlike the painter, you cannot wilfully mix colors, but must choose from already "mixed" veneers. Nevertheless there are veneers for dark brown hair (walnut burr), for sky effects (avodire and others), for sea effects, shadows, and reflections. These are all available locally. As a serious craftsman you must study them and slowly acquire a good selection. After you have collected at least from thirty to sixty different types of veneers, make your own little gamut of color graduations in the different shades. Some woods have a blackish tint, some reddish, and some brownish.

Little by little make a 1- x 2-inch collection of veneer samples, and as you proceed you will learn not only the colors but the characteristics of the wood veneers. Such knowledge is invaluable to the inlay craftsman.

In the trade, unusual veneers are called "freak" veneers. But in fact they are so beautiful that they deserve another name. Regardless of name, all veneers are beautiful. A veneer called "freak" does not create a freak work.

But to return to our picture panel: once the sketch is traced, trace a line ½ inch larger than the sketch size all around the picture, using black carbon paper. Tape 1/16-inch plywood from those lines onward—that is, ½-inch strips. Your working veneers can be butted against the strips when you trace them. The sketch can always be flapped back after each tracing. You can work with jigsaw (or knife) each time and then return the veneer, butting it into exactly the same place for a new tracing.

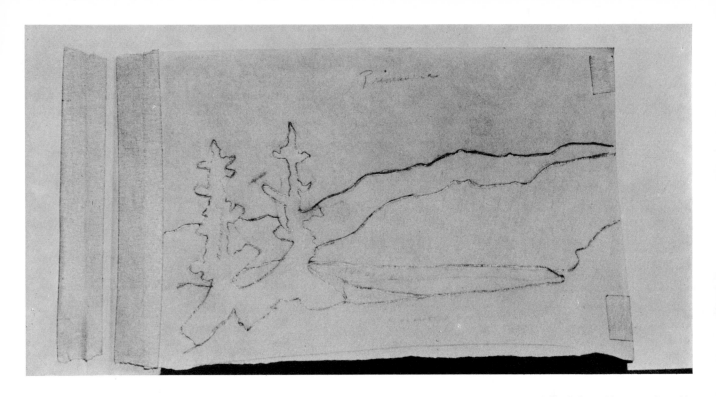

2. Sketch shown with veneers to be used for its various sections.

Opposite Page

1. A basically simple landscape picture is drawn on bond paper with pencil or ink. The drawing is taped on its left side to a wooden board ($\frac{1}{4}$-inch poplar) that will act as a base for the finished inlaid picture. The drawing is traced through carbon paper onto all sections of veneer that will be cut to shape and then glued onto the board. The wooden board is 1 inch wider than the drawing on all sides. Before the drawing is traced onto veneer strips, a $\frac{1}{2}$-inch outline is made on the board all around the picture. A raised edge, $\frac{3}{4}$-inch wide, is glued all around the outer edge of the board. As the picture progresses, all working veneer pieces are butted against this surrounding strip.

3. The veneer selected for sky and mountains is placed under the sketch and traced upon. The veneer is cut with a jigsaw (or a knife), taped together, and butted against the upper, raised edge of the plywood block.

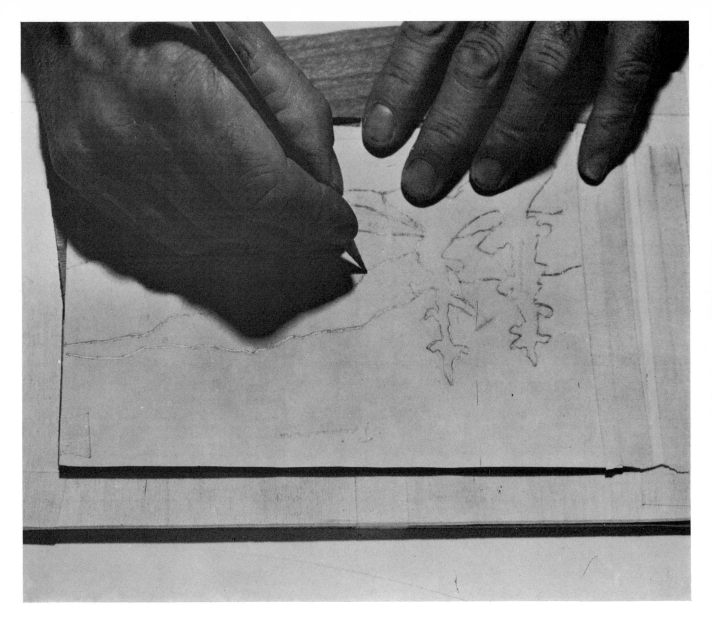

4. The central part of the landscape is traced
onto a new veneer placed under the drawing.

5. The veneer strip for step 4, showing the
lines traced on its surface. It is now cut on
the jigsaw and then fitted into place with
the already cut veneer pieces.

6. Three pieces of veneer already cut with a
fourth part being put in place for next
tracing and cut.

7. Lower veneer sections. Two cut veneers
are taped in place, traced from drawing, and
then cut.

54

8. Fifth veneer section is placed on the board for tracing, cutting, and then fitting into place.

9. Another veneer is put in place for tracing from drawing.

10. Tracing on veneer from step 9.

11. All horizontal veneers for the landscape
are cut and taped together.

12. Reverse side of taped panel indicating
how the various pieces of veneer are care-
fully interlocked.

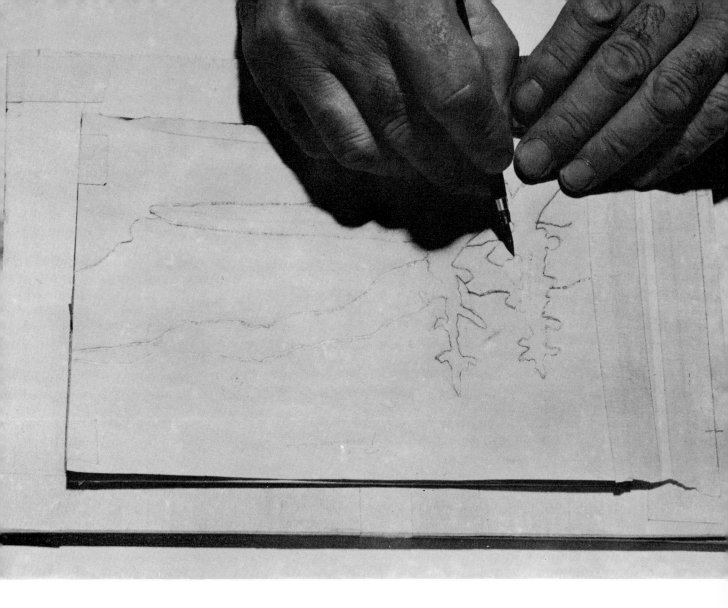

13. First vertical tracing on veneer, the trees.

14. Trees are cut out and taped into place.
Veneers underneath them are first removed
so that the trees will be flush with the panel
surface.

15. Untaped side of panel showing the completed picture.

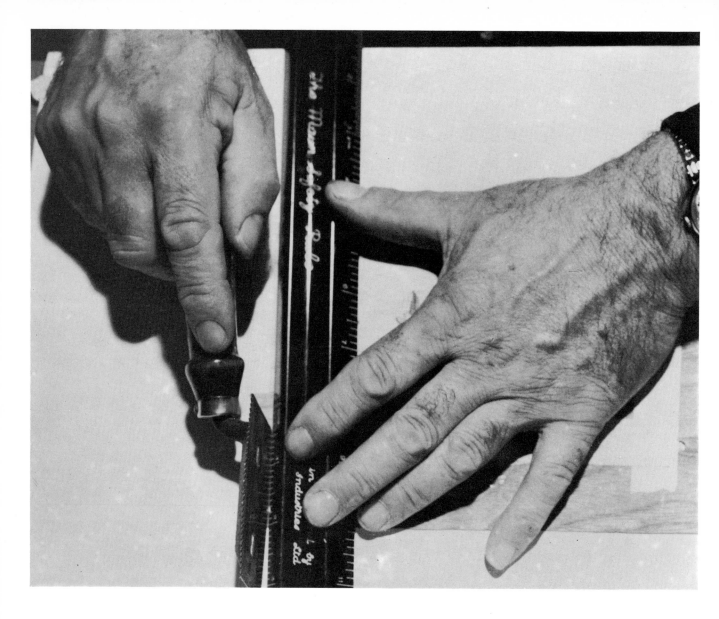

16. Trimming edges of veneer panel with a
veneer saw to prepare it for a border.

17. One part of border put in place, taped to panel on reverse side.

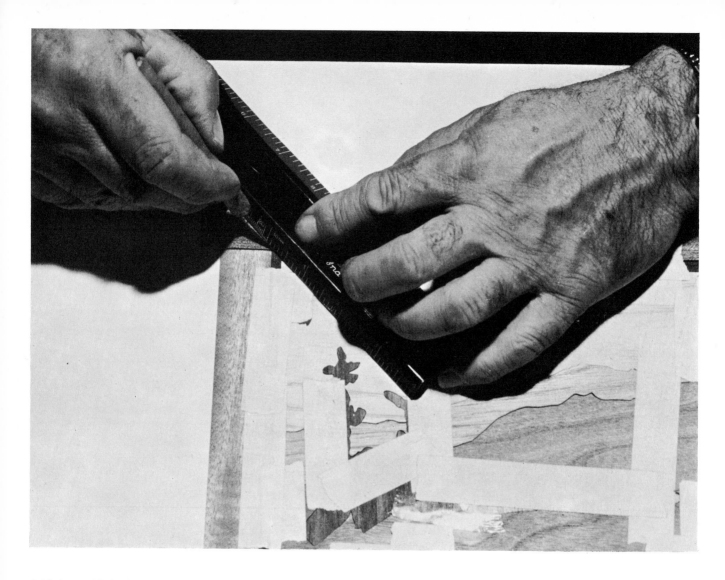

18. All pieces used for border are taped in place. The corners are being mitred with a knife for joining properly at angles.

19. Veneer frame is cut and taped into place. Everything is glued together as in coaster project.

20. Finished picture panel and frame.

Snow Scene by Joseph Forgione. The panel
is 8 x 12 inches with its broad inlaid frame.
The white snow is depicted with holly veneer.

Beached Boat by Cappiello Bonaventura. Scenic panel, 14½ x 10½ inches, inlaid with cut wood pieces of contrasting values and grains that create the illusion of three-dimensional space, a variety of surface textures, and an active ocean surf.

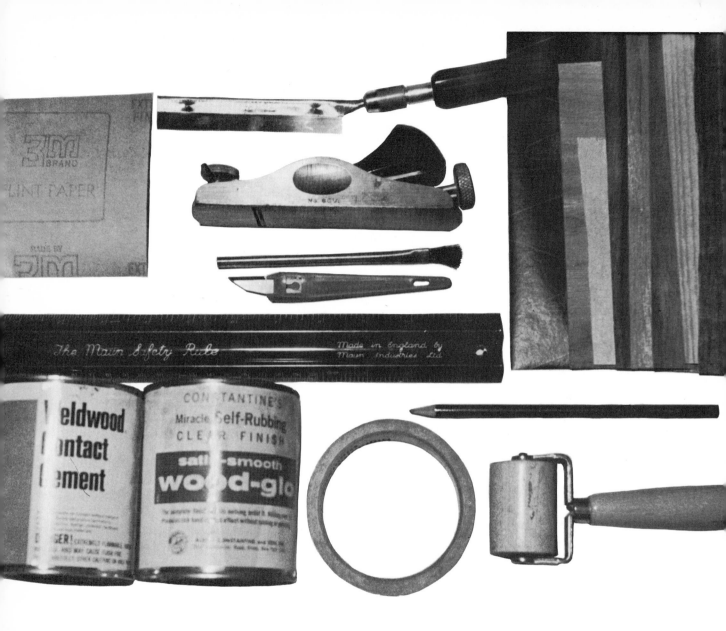

Students' tools. *Above:* sandpaper, razor saw, block plane, brush, hand knife, veneers, metal ruler. *Below:* contact cement, varnish, tape, pencil, seam roller.

7.
Student Projects

In technique and materials wood inlay is an ideal art and craft for the young student. Wood is a familiar medium with which the young artist can create durable work. According to a teacher's instruction and the student's imagination, wood-inlay design can range all the way from naturalistic to abstract. The technique of wood inlay as demonstrated here provides an excellent introduction to the use of simple hand tools and the principles of creative design by the individual. Once students have mastered the basic, 6- x 6-inch block, they can expand the experience gained to work with increased complexity and on a grander scale.

The art illustrated in this chapter was made by high-school students of art teacher Josephine Russo of Jersey City, New Jersey. When easy-to-use tools were decided upon, the students were provided with kits and a choice of various veneers.

The program was organized by Joseph Forgione, who adapted it to the learning skills required and the age and previous experience of the students. Generally the projects were organized in the following manner.

Project Procedure

After a close examination of the veneer sheets, students made preliminary drawings in pen or pencil of the design they would create with wood. The designs were then transferred to plywood work boards with the aid of carbon paper. Small pieces of veneer were cut to correspond with the various design elements, and taped together over the drawing.

When the design was complete and fully taped together, it was pulled loose from the work board. One side of the design is completely taped together; the side formerly pressed against the work board is visible and free of tape. It is this latter, free side that was then cemented to a block cut to the size, 6 x 6 inches, of the design. When using rubber cement, *both* surfaces to be joined were brushed with the cement and pressed firmly together after the thick liquid had dried to a tacky consistency.

When the veneer design cemented to the block was dry, all tape was removed from its surface to reveal the original design begun with a preliminary drawing. Strips of veneer were then cut to measure, and cemented to the bottom and sides of the design block. Finally, the design surface was finely sanded and then varnished, in order to help preserve the design and to emphasize the textures of the cut veneer elements.

1. Original drawing and veneer strips selected for project.

2. Design transformed to working board,
¼-inch thick plywood. Wood was selected
because of small size of design, 6 x 6 inches.

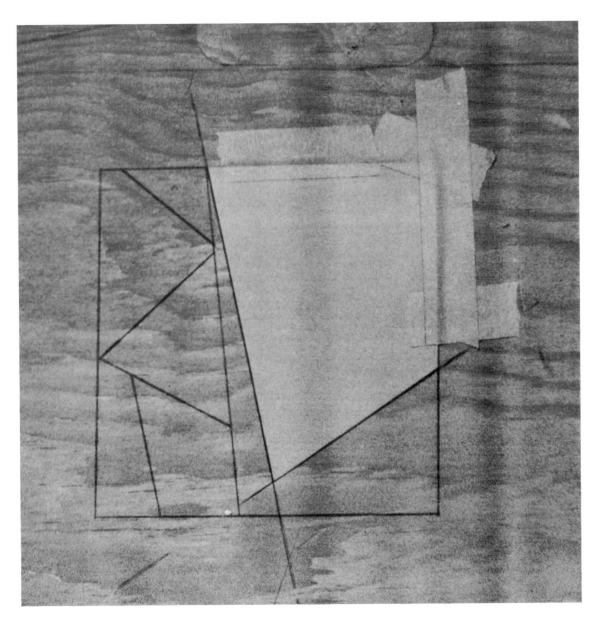

3. First piece of veneer for design cut in place – right on the design – and taped in place.

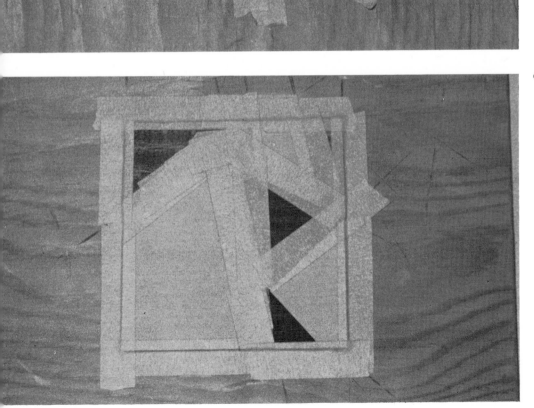

5. Other design pieces cut and taped in place.

6. Entire design taped in place.

7. Design (right) with taped part underneath and $\frac{1}{4}$-inch block onto which taped design will be glued.

8. Applying contact cement both to untaped side of design and block surface. Allow drying time for cement until it is tacky, about 20 minutes in room of normal temperature.

81

9. Tape has been removed from upper side of design. Here the excess wood border is being trimmed off with razor saw.

10. Trimming strip of veneer cemented to back surface of block. The seam roller is used for all applications of cement.

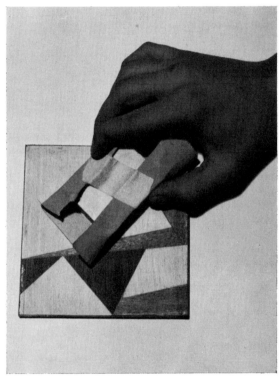

11. Strips of veneer to be applied to the four sides of the design are cemented on in same manner.

12. Sanding with fine sandpaper wrapped around a block of wood.

13. Varnish and brush used to finish inlay design block.

1. Original drawing of design on paper.

2. Transferring drawing to working board with carbon paper.

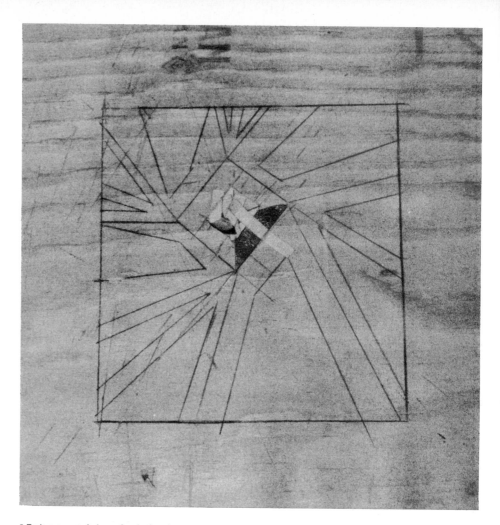

3. Taping veneer to design on drawing board.

Opposite Page

4. Midway through taping veneer strips to drawing board.

5. All veneer pieces taped together.

6. Veneer design completely taped and ready
for cementing to block.

H

7. Applying rubber cement on untaped side
of design and to face of block.

8. Trimming off excess block with razor saw.

9. Back of block showing veneer surface cemented to it.

10. Cementing four sides to be applied to block.

Opposite Page

Four finished block designs, including Projects 1 and 2.

Commercial poster, 38 x 24 inches, by
Milton Glaser. Complex illusion of a cup-
board containing books, astronomic models,
amphora, and a typewriter at odd angles.
This work of graphic art emulates pure
wood inlay, for it was created with a familiar
modern medium, wood-textured, contact-
paper strips.

8.
Contemporary Wood Inlay

In some ways the contemporary craftsman continues the techniques of the
traditional wood-inlay artist. Designers
are still fascinated by ancient geometric
pattern and the creation of figurative
panels. In all examples, the smooth inlaid
surface with its emphasis on variety in
value, hue, and grain relates to each past
period, regardless of its time and place.

Yet ours is a unique age, emphasizing
function and mass production, elements
that affect the artist—and everyone else.
Unlike most earlier examples, seldom
today can the wood-inlay craftsman rely
on wealthy or royal patrons who will call
upon him to decorate their splendid
homes or offices with one-of-a-kind
panels, doors or furniture.

Today's wood craftsman relies primarily on his own talents and aims.
The results are occasionally similar, as
in all the arts, but bear the useful and
lively stamp of our changeable time.
As examples in this chapter reveal, no
matter what its design or function, wood
inlay is still a highly creative and in-
ventive form of art.

Coffee table, 40 inches long, by Frank Rohloff, 1963. Naturalistic and free-design shamrock shapes of dark walnut are laid into a white top to form a lively value-contrast design for a lengthy top.

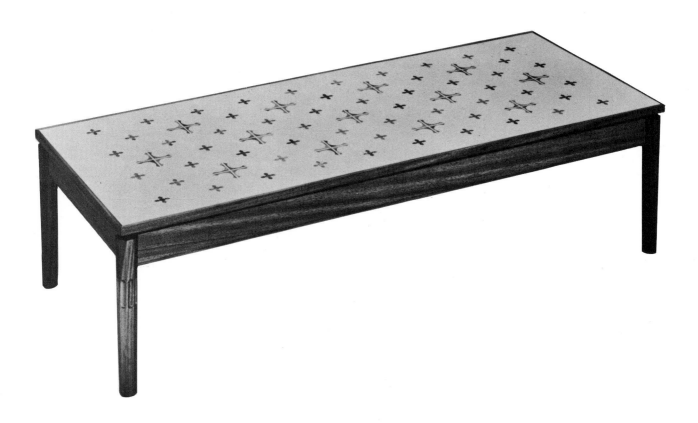

Pendant, 2 x 1½ inches, by Irving Potter, 1963. An uneven miniature checker design of beefwood and camphorwood for personal adornment. The light squares, further inlaid with figurative lines and circles, add a sprightly note. (Reproduced courtesy of *Craft Horizons*.)

Table top with circular wood-inlay pattern of repeated geometric wood elements by Frank Rohloff (photograph by Richard Fish.)

Wall hanging plate, 3½ x 5 inches, by Irving Potter, 1963. Inlaid circles in squares provide a simple but bold series of optical targets for a miniature wall decoration.

Chess board by Arthur Strom. Walnut and birch squares (1¾ inches square) are joined solid, rather than with veneers, so that the surface is playable on both sides. The board was finished with penetrating oil. (Reproduction courtesy American Craftsmen's Council.)

Tables by Frank Rohloff. Walnut and polyester white table is 36 inches square, dark table 48 inches, both made in 1969. Walnut wood designs are laid in white and black polyester resin blocks to combine traditional and contemporary media with a repeated geometric design.

Folding square table, coffee table, and cube by Frank Rohloff. White polyester inlaid with evenly spaced walnut design elements. The right-angle placement of the inlaid walnut captures the square and rectangular shapes of the furniture.

Wood-inlay block for a floor, teak, 12 x 12 inches, 1972. In repeated combination, commercial inlay blocks, although mass-produced, create a modern version of the traditional, geometrically designed parquet floor. Such blocks are easily made by hand for covering floors as well as mantles and table tops. (Reproduced courtesy Designed Wood Flooring Center, Inc.)